What People are Saying

That was inspiring! Thank you for sharing your poetry with us. You inspired me to be grateful for everything. You taught me that every day is a gift.

Kade K.

You come up with great poems.

Evan J.

Even though I wasn't there, by the looks of the class when I came back, it told me that you are a professional poet...my favorite part of poetry is the relaxation and the feeling it gives you.

Jordan F.

The whole class loved your poems. A kid named Kaely started to cry during one of the poems...one was sad, but I liked what it had to say.

Taisha

You could have been at the barber shop making money, but instead you came to our class to teach poetry. You are the best for sharing your poetry.

Adam E.

Your poetry is very beautiful. I can tell it came from your heart. I hope you share it with the world. Everybody will love it.

Sara

You took the time for us. You could have been writing more poems. You could have been relaxing at home. I think you get what I'm saying.

Zola C.

1

You inspired me to make my own poems with the feelings from my heart. Mr. Tony taught me how to be a true poet.

Cloe

Since you shared your personal experiences with us, I might start sharing my experiences with the world.

Konner

Your poems are like a joy to my world.

Aubrey

If you had never come to our school and inspired me, my mother probably would never have gotten a Mother's Day poem. Thank you for inspiring me.

Nathan

POEMS

FROM THE

HEART

Personal Feelings Shared
To be of help to others in need

by

Tony Cammilleri

Tony Cammilleri

To all of you who have been so kind
in reading my work
and sharing it with others

Table of Contents

Forward

For over forty years, Tony has been our friend.
Throughout our friendship, we have witnessed his
unselfish service to others. It is his gift. People are
important to him and he demonstrates that by uplifting,
encouraging, helping and love his fellow men.
Sometimes, it's by a smile, a song, sharing a story or
two, or making a visit to the lonely, sick or
disheartened.

After the death of Marilyn, his beloved wife of sixty-two
years, he started writing poems as ideas come to him.
He has felt inspired to share them with others. From
school children to the elderly and others in between, his
simple poems touch hearts. Powerful messages within
each poem teach and inspire.

Thank you, Tony, for this gift of your heart.

Diane Johnson

About LOSS

and LOVE

and HOPE

and SURVIVING

Remembering With Hope

We shed tears when we're happy
and when we have sorrow
We take inventory of blessings
And keep looking forward to tomorrow

My wife went to the Lord in September
Remembering the wonderful life we shared
The loneliness that can't be explained to others
Friends, relatives, sisters and brothers who cared

My heart goes out to others who loved for a short time
those who've died
Lost suddenly due to an illness or accident
Or even suicide

People say that time and prayers
will help you heal
I'm sure this is true
but no one knows just how you feel.

Recently in church I was touched
by our pastor's sermon and I shed a tear
There was a tap on my shoulder
and I received tissues from someone so dear

You think you're alone
looking into space
But there's always someone near
that can read your face

We mortals have no idea the path
that lies ahead for me and you.
Reach out to our Lord
There's so much that lies ahead for us to do

January 2016

A Message from Heaven

I woke up at 2:00 a.m. to write a poem
as you went to the Lord one year ago today
My subconscious worked overtime
guiding my hand with words showing the way

Who would have known how a life can change
it's so hard to explain
It was so difficult see the one I love
go through so much pain

Now with our Lord your suffering is gone
and you're in a much better place
The years we spent together were wonderful
and I will always miss your smiling face

Being survivors we must remember
the wonderful lives we shared together
Thoughts go through my mind
could there ever be another

Life has its ups and downs
We follow our hearts and endure
We pray that for what took our loved ones
they one day find a cure

I thank God for the friends
that were sent my way
For their support
I thank God each and every day

Embrace the void you now have
without your mate as you must do
There's still so much that lies ahead
for me and you

Our life is a journey that isn't complete
Reach out to the Lord
give thanks
there are friends yet to meet

September 2016

What Love Means to Me

Love in the dictionary says strong feelings
a kiss or an embrace
To me it means doing little things
that put a smile on your loved one's face

The hugs and kisses, yes,
they mean a lot
Our actions and kindnesses
are what love's all about

Going through life's ups and downs
We were put to the test
Our strong feelings for each other
We always thought of the best

Holding hands, a warm embrace
and a smile or two
Our love wasn't hidden
It definitely did show through

We were there for each other
when there was a need
Mutual support we shared
It was as we agreed

Thank God for watching over us
through the years
There were many times
we did shed some tears

When I see what we shared
all the blessing of love
I look up and smile
and thank God above

May 2016

About HOLIDAYS

and the SEASONS of LIFE

Memories of Valentine's Past

Valentine's Day
a special time of the year
I gave you a card, flowers or a trinket
to my love so dear

How very strange not to have you
physically with me today
But you'll always be in my heart
there's no other way

Your hugs and kisses
and holding hands too
I opened your car door
and did little things for you

Never enough things you're willing to do
for someone you love
I wish you were here with me
instead of looking down from above

Last year I got on my knees, held your hand
and sang you a song
Those fond memories will stay in my heart
who knows for how long

The loneliness
is so very hard to explain
We spent sixty-two years together
so I shouldn't complain

There are so many couples
who don't share our love
We were so lucky to have one another
I thank God above

Valentine's Day, February 14, 2016

What
Christmas
Means
to
Me

Christmas is a special time of year
when families get together
To celebrate Jesus' birth
and share with one another
this happy time of the year
with beautiful songs to hear
Choirs unite their voices
so pleasant to the ear
adorn our homes with lights
of all types, colors and such
An atmosphere of happiness
that always means so much
We Christians know Jesus
is the reason for the season
feelings of love are spread
to the world for this reason
We look up to the heavens
and thank God for His son
We've been blessed for our journey
that has just begun

October 2016

Remembrance at Christmas

Holidays
never seem
the same
my loved one isn't there
I try so hard to enjoy
friends and relatives
but there's that empty chair
the joy we shared at holidays
I can't put into words
smiles and laughter
and the sharing of food and drink
all the "thank you"s were heard
I wasn't going to put up lights
Well the Christmas tree went up
and decorations too to my delight
to not decorate our house you would have been upset with me
I followed your blueprints of where things should be
with ornaments on the tree I turned on the lights every night
knowing that you'd want me to be enjoying the decorations
and turning on Christmas tree lights
reminded me
of you

April 2016,
looking back on our first Christmas apart

This Year I'm Spending Time with Jesus
A NEW YEAR Reflection

This year I'm spending time with Jesus
best done by joining in His deeds
In my mind I see Jesus with outstretched arms
giving hope and meeting needs

Jesus set the bar so high
for me and other sinners to attain
We open our hearts to Him and to people
who've lost jobs, loved ones or felt other pain

As followers we go out of our way
to show love for one another
At Christmas we do even more
by celebrating God's gift like no other

The blessings of love and forgiveness
this feeling we need to share
We reach out to those who need love
and smile to show we care

Life is so short
There's so much to do
Teachings from Jesus' life
Lived and spoken by me and you

Look to the heavens and ask our Lord
He'll gladly show us the way
As we do great deeds for others
we spend time with Jesus today

December 2016

We Must Share God's Love
A NEW YEAR Reflection

Another year has come and gone
Looking back at what I could have done
My resolution this year will be
To do more for others kind and free
What a wonderful world we would see
If we just loved one another

My writings are a gift, so I've been told
I will strive to share with the young and old
Giving school kids the chance at a healthy start
My goal is to touch each mind and heart
For this is what sets us as Christians apart
We must share the blessing

Our world today is upside down
A smiling God is caused to frown
We must spread a hope so bright
To those who've seen no love in sight
Assure them there's a shining light
Coming down from above

There are so many unaware
They think there's no one here to care
The doors of heaven are open wide
Eternal life lies just inside
And for today true love abides
Our grief and sorrow answered

We're blessed that in our land of freedom
We can worship the Father as we see Him
What lies ahead each coming day
Is a taste of heaven on the way
The final goal, I must say,
To see God face to face.

December 2016

The Miracle of Easter

God's love for us sinners is hard to explain
He sent His one and only son
to die for us
and to endure our pain

Dying on a cross for not committing a crime
it's so hard to understand
A crown of thorns placed on his head
and nails driven through his hands

When dying on that cross there was thunder
lightning and the ground shook
Daylight became darkness
mourners covered their eyes and didn't want to look

The centurions placed a large stone
at the entrance of Jesus tomb and didn't care
Days later the mourners came to pray
but the stone was rolled away and Jesus wasn't there

The joy that Jesus has risen
echoed loud and clear
This wonderful miracle quickly
was spread to many ears

It was God's plan all along
for Jesus to rise from the dead
That's why we celebrate Easter
and look to the sky and wonder what lies ahead

April 2016

The Gift of Life

Springtime is such a wonderful time of the year
flowers bloom
birds return to roost
and their singing is music to my ear

       the birth of birds
       elk and deer
       God made it possible for us
       to enjoy the miracle of birth

We must enjoy this gift
open our eyes
and thank heaven and earth

       People who feel
       life on earth hasn't been fair
       my heart goes out to them
       because God's love is always there

Probably they never had hugs
and weren't even told that they were loved
happiness they could enjoy if knowing
God was calling for them from above

       Grace
       We're taught about God's grace
       and at the end of our life,
       we'll see His holy face.

       April 2016

MOM

Giving birth to a child
A mother suffers pain
The joy of seeing this beautiful life
Means mothers would do it again

Moms take care of our sniffles
Mend our bruises and such
Listening to our troubles she'll give advice
Because she loves us so much

We can't thank moms enough for their care
They've loved us in so every way
Though often we're just not aware
Every May we celebrate Mother's Day

I praise you for just being who you are
Again, I give you my love
To have a mom is a blessing
I do thank God above

We can do things for moms throughout the year
Instead of waiting 'til May
So any time it's good to celebrate
HAPPY MOTHER'S DAY

May 2017

Dad

We celebrate Mother's Day in May
In June we didn't forget you Dad
We give so many praises to moms
But we also gave you a day

You were always there as Mr. Fixit
Having the task of making sure that there
Was always air in our bike's tires
And whatever else needed repair

Without you in our life
We would have missed so much
You encouraged us to set goals and high standards
Using your pleasant touch

We've seen those that don't have dads
In their lives due to divorce, or dad is dead
Our hearts go out to those who have that empty spot
And could have had joy instead

Thank you for splitting your time with our sporting events
And whatever our endeavors were
It meant so much that you could have said "no"
But you were always there

HAPPY FATHER'S DAY

May 2017

About GOD

and JESUS

and the LIFE OF LOVE

God's Grace

What does grace mean to me?
We must forgive as it should be

In the workplace jealous thoughts arise
To compete for jobs is no surprise

Forgiving is not an easy task
And wanting advice who should we ask?

We need to ask God for what to do
His answer? what would you like done to you

Our thoughts and actions are put to the test
Reach out, thank God and think only of the best

The hurt we've felt we must forgive
Think only of tomorrow and the life we must live

So many choices I want to shout
These thoughts are what grace is all about

May 2016

God's Gift to the World

Once
upon a Holy Day
angels a baby did bring
to Mary, Joseph and all mankind
the joy and warmth
to make us sing

Wise men
traveled day and night
to a strange and faraway place
When they arrived they were greeted
by the holy face
This Little Child
Led them far
as they were led
by a shining star

This Gift
in his
short
lived
years
did things remembered in our hearts
and spread to many open ears
He died
on a
cross
for all
to see
when we feel
we have suffered
none has suffered as he

Even in his dying words
He loved us sinners true
He said "Forgive them, Father
for they know not what they do"

December 1965

The Key to Heaven

The book *Believe* shows the way
to be more like Jesus every day
On the cover a picture of a key
The gates of heaven open for me
With compassion
we share with the
ones who are lost
They too can be saved
Jesus covered the cost
Assure those
who doubt
that heaven's
the place
After living our lives
see the smile of God's face
For now we offer total surrender
A daily quest to help one another
Patience
kindness
gentleness
will show
The joy of
relationship
with a God
we can know
Assured our
souls will be
blessed forever
In a place

where we all
can share
fellowship
together
For now we see
those blessings in part
At church we give praise
as the Spirit touches hearts
And we learn how to love
Which sets us apart
BELIEVE

March 2017

Sun's Beauty

Sitting in my recliner each night
I enjoy the sunset
With the sun's rays glistening through the trees
and the beauty of this event so splendid
If only others could see that the sun is amazing
It warms the soil to make plants grow
It gives light instead of darkness for all of us below
God has created this cycle not just to warm the earth
But also our souls
As Christians we know that nature's beauty
Must be shared with us all
Going outside with a camera
Thinking I can capture the beauty in a picture
It's disappointing that justice can't be done
To the beauty of Mother Nature
I find it very difficult to put into words
God's blessing we all share
What a great feeling we have
Knowing that Jesus is everywhere

2017

About the GIFTS

of FRIENDSHIP

and WRITING

Friends

Life on this earth can be a treat
God has given us friends to meet
Each day has its ups and downs
Let's make smiles instead of frowns

Trust in our faith and we will learn
by believing in Jesus we get joy in return
We mortals have such a short time to live
Today we have so much to give

Our thoughts
and what we say and do
Can bring happiness
to more than a few

A very wise woman once said to me
"You can never have too many friends"
I've found her simple words to be true
So I'll make sure that thought never ends

Caring

We just don't know
　　how much people care
　　　　All the kindnesses shown
　　　　　　while we're unaware

So much loving and giving
　　thought and prayer
　　　　Our trials and burdens
　　　　　　they're willing to share

We take our health
　　for granted each day
　　　　The problems of others
　　　　　　seem so far away

But our health can be taken
　　away so quickly
　　　　I've seen this happen
　　　　　　to Marilyn personally

The care the hospital
　　staff has given
　　　　So overboard
　　　　　　we felt like we were "livin'"

It's not fun in a hospital
　　bed for days
　　　　That's why they work so hard
　　　　　　toward short stays

We thank doctors, nurses
　　and rehab, too
　　　　When we leave
　　　　　　we will give praise to you

God's Blessings

Friendships are a blessing
    we must embrace
And thank God for this gift
    so hard to replace

        There are times we need help
        but don't want to ask
      If friends know they are needed
        they'd handle the task

It's terrible to think that
    without a friend or two
Some miss this blessing
    for me and for you

      There are many opportunities
        for us to take
      We need to think positive
        about choices we make

Be optimistic when seeing
    what lies ahead
The temptation is to think
    "no way" instead

      Questions rise
        about achievers
      They say it was luck
        but they were believers

When we ask for help
    from God above
We're amazingly showered
    with hope and love

We must go through life
        thinking only the best
Be humble and gracious
        He'll take care of the rest

Feelings I Must Write

Thoughts come to me day and night
Something tells me I need to write

God gives gifts of which we're not aware
There are so many riches we need to share

Why I'm wanting to write is a mystery to me
Feelings awakened by my surroundings

Make it easy for me to see
The joy of friendships kind and free

Mother Nature and friends mean so much
Their inspiration such a wonderful touch

Life can be a great journey we must embrace
Doing things for others puts a smile on their face

People I know go out of their way
to shop for those who can never repay

Or phone just to say hello
They wouldn't think of saying no

The joy they get from helping others
A life filled with sisters and brothers

That's what life should be all about
The wonder of helping someone out

God, I'm sure, has a smile on His face
For the helper He lends His quiet praise

Seeing us doing these wonderful deeds
Like Him Who cares for people's needs

May 2016

For Some People I Know

Harvey Speck
(Mr. Wonderful)

Harvey
    I'm sure
        is looking down at us today

He's happy
    we're sharing
        his life stories from day to day

It's great
    we're sharing
        his humor and his wit

There were times
    I didn't understand
        his one-liners, I must admit

It was fun
    knowing Harvey
        I'm sure that is shared by us all

His return
    phone messages
        would end with "it's Mr. Wonderful!"

This poem
    is going to be short
        as there's so much I'd like to say

You'll be missed
    but will be remembered
        in our hearts each and every day.

To the Wonderful 4th Graders

Doing a class for you
        has been such a pleasure
the sharing of my poetry
        and laughter

I will always treasure
        I touched your minds and your heart
Your future seems so bright
        and this is just the start

Please go through life
        thinking of the best
Your life is just beginning
        so don't let your minds rest

Life on this earth
        is such a treat
Thank God for each day
        and the friends you will meet

May 2016

Life's Legacy

Politicians pass laws and new regulations
     to give themselves a legacy
These actions were not done from the heart
     as we can see

I've observed a wonderful family
     for over forty years to my delight
their family grew from children to grandchildren
     what a pleasant sight

I saw them mold their children with love
     and were told "you must be responsible"
This took both of them
     being a role model

The children were taught the value
     of faith and family
They were told to endure the day to day challenges
     and face reality

Mom and daughters do their annual retreat
     enjoying an opera or a stage show
This bond they have is not as a mom
     but as friends with a glow

Dad taught his family the love
     of Mother Nature's gift for me and you
The mountains, rivers and their beauty
     and how to catch a fish or two

The years go by watching your children
mature before our eyes
The love and praise the children
gave their parents wasn't a surprise

When Mom and Dad leave this Earth they'll smile
and look down from above at their family
and say it's a wonderful sight to see
The family they left on Earth is their
wonderful legacy

Dedicated to my very dear friends,
Kimber and Dianne Johnson

Our Dear Leone

Northwood is blessed to have you
    for fifteen years
        teaching the Holy Book

The dedication and preparation
    no one knows
        just how long that took

You've shared the word with so many
    you're not aware
        just how many

The twinkle in your eyes and your hugs
    mean so much
        You have no idea how many
          you've touched

Northwood women have spread the word
    Women have come from other churches
        and said you're a blessing

You have a gift for sharing the Word
    All the words, feelings and thoughts
        have been heard

We're happy you only
    gave up the library task
        to replace you we'd not know
        whom to ask

We look forward to Tuesdays that lie ahead
    There are so many scriptures and
        verses we haven't yet read
        We thank you

The Prayer Quilt

I woke up this morning at three a.m.
thinking of you, women from Northwood
about the quilt you had sewn
Your time and prayers were felt so deeply
We could not have known
Your quilt was presented to Marilyn
At the hospital by Trudy Blier
Marilyn and I felt your thoughtfulness
And your prayers as if you were there
Smiles and tears she felt
Knowing there were so many that did care
The quilt warmed her frail body
And gave solace to her soul
I know you ladies do this to give joy and happiness
As this is your goal
Your kindness will always be remembered
Whenever I see the quilt
You touched Marilyn deeply
As there was a gleam in her eyes I must admit
The quilt was presented to her approximately
Two years ago today
I want you to know your thoughtfulness
Is in my heart and will never fade away
I thank you ladies of Northwood

Sincerely,
Tony Cammilleri
August, 2017

ABOUT our BOOK COVER
Don't Ever Give Up

Don't ever give up when you're looking for something special. It may be where you never dreamed possible.

I was looking for that special sunset or sunrise photo for the cover. I spent two days looking through the many photo albums my wife had put together in our sixty-plus years of marriage. I was going through the last three albums with no luck and ready to give up.

Tucked away in the back of the cabinet, among those last three albums, I saw a grocery bag. That bag was filled with the photos that were never put in albums.

I started going through envelopes hoping I could find that special picture. Yes, I was so disappointed and was ready to give up. In the bottom of that bag was an assortment of loose negatives, paid receipts and blank note paper. I figured I might as well sort through all this stuff.

As I started going through this assortment of stuff, I saw the picture that was going to be our cover. I was so excited. I kept saying, "Wow, this is it!" I can't put into words my excitement after seeing that picture when I was ready to give up.

I took that picture many years ago on the water of Lake Havasu in Arizona. The thought of this picture waiting for me, so it could be shared with many, was astounding.

I've come to believe that we all have a destiny waiting to be filled. I know deep in my heart that this picture was there waiting for me. This whole cycle of events in my life, along with my writings of poetry, has touched me deeply.

My wonderful friends have encouraged me to keep writing. I've been blessed to have friends who have helped me put this project together and I know this is a blessing from above.

We should never give up when trying to find the special photo, or event, or that special person in our lives.

There's tomorrow, next week or the next hour when our wish could come true.

Don't ever give up!

ACKNOWLEDGEMENTS

Thanks to one of my dearest friends, Diane Johnson, for typing all of my writings.

The graphic design on the cover was done by Dr. Gerald Harper. Thanks.

My sincere appreciation to Keith Potter for helping me publish this book. His experience and creative ability have been a blessing. Without his help, I might have just had a dream of *wanting* to publish a book. Many, many thanks.

I must also thank my many friends and relatives who encouraged me to keep writing.

Still More Critical Acclaim...

You chose good topics. You placed all of your writing in the name of Jesus, and I loved that. I understood your feelings and emotions put to writing.

Malachi

You inspired me to look at and admire nature.

Chloe C.

Your poems are funny, sad, happy, loving and caring. I bet it took a long time for you to do the poems. We all loved them.

Adriana C.

After you came to our class, I went home and wrote a poem.

Bailey

Keep working on your poem book!

Bryannah

I liked your poems and I liked your hairdo.

Patrick

You made the class feel special when you read the poems to us. I felt special!

Abby

Now I write poems all by myself.

Cade M.

You spoke with a lot of expression. Your poems are heartfelt.
> Cherokee

Your stories and poetry made me think poetry is cool.
> Adrianna

You were very, very, very funny. Now I write poems everywhere I go.
> Breisa

You made me want to share my feelings to other people. I used to keep it in my head.
> Rhiannon

I could tell you took your time on every single one of them.

> Kaley T.

I love poetry because of you.
> Zoie

You said stuff about losing your wife and I remembered losing my grandma. I used to think poetry was overrated, but you taught me it's way more fun than I thought.
> Karli M.

Made in the USA
Columbia, SC
21 October 2022

69788463R00043